Tabitha and The Jets

Julius Dogwood

Copyright © 2025 by Julius Dogwood

All rights reserved.

No portion of this book may be reproduced in any form without written permission from the publisher or author, except as permitted by U.S. copyright law.

Contents

A note from Julius Dogwood   1

Foreword by Ryan Millar   3

Dedication   5

1. Saying Goodbye   6
2. Welcome to Summerland   12
3. First Visit to School   19
4. The Radio Station   27
5. First Day Rhythms   31
6. Saturday at the Rink   36
7. The View from Above   42
8. The Big Mistake   47
9. The Swap Meet   51
10. Practice, Practice, Practice   56
11. Snarl Power   59

12. Time to Choose	66
13. Game Time	71
Epilogue – Finding Her Edge	78
14. Glossary	81
A Couple More Things	85

A note from Julius Dogwood

The best stories grow like fruit trees—from sturdy roots of truth, nourished by imagination, and reaching toward something sweeter. This tale sprouted from my memories of Summerland, British Columbia—though not exactly this Summerland, and not quite these events. But memory plays tricks, especially when fortified with imagination. Like the orchards of the Okanagan, these events have been carefully tended to; part memory, part invention, and wholly a labor of love.

Writing this book from my home far away in time and space from my childhood, I wanted young readers to get a feeling for small-town Canadian life. Not just the facts and info, the feelings.

By the way: the Murphy family might be fictional but, then again, they might not be. They're the kind of family you find in any small Canadian town where kids are discovering who they are, parents are remembering who they used to be, and everyone's just trying their best to make it all work... somehow.

Julius Dogwood
Somewhere in Europe, 2025

Foreword by Ryan Millar

I don't think about Summerland much.

But when Julius Dogwood first shared this manuscript with me, I felt an immediate connection to its world. That's because, as it happens, I too grew up in Summerland. What a small world—and what a small town. I recognized not just the landmarks but the rhythm of the place, things I can appreciate much more from a distance, as it turns out.

What Dogwood has crafted here is more than just another children's story. Like Stuart McLean's beloved "Dave and Morley stories" (as my nephew Morgan calls them), the Summerland Stories capture something essentially Canadian in their exploration of family life. The Murphys, with their perfect mix of support and silliness, represent something both highly specific and deeply universal about growing up in Canada.

I love how this book balances the everyday with the extraordinary. Yes, there are hockey games and figure skating competitions, but there's also the quiet moments of finding friends and finding your place.

I myself couldn't wait to leave Summerland after high school, for I had big ideas and big dreams. But now, from the distance of middle age (and approximately 7,500 kilometres) I can much better appreciate its charms.

Julius, and the Murphy family, as well as the rest of the characters in this story, sure help with that.

Ryan Millar
Amsterdam, 2025

Dedication

For Neve and Arya, two supremely awesome Canadian girls.

Chapter One

Saying Goodbye

"MIIIIIIIIIKE!"

Tabitha's scream cut through the quiet Moose Jaw morning. Her competition figure skates – the ones she'd earned with last season's bronze medal – were propped against the house instead of packed in the moving van where they belonged.

"What now?" Dad sighed, pulling their grey Ford station wagon off to the side of Fairford Street and turning the hazard lights on. He knew something was up.

"I packed my skates," Tabitha mumbled, "I know I did."

"Strange how they got out there then," Mike said, tapping innocently on his window. At thirteen, he had perfected the art of looking completely unconvincing.

"Well, we've gone 100 feet, good time for a break," Mom said, wearily.

They both turned in their seats and fixed their eyes on their middle child, who was trying (and failing) to hide a smirk.

Dad raised an eyebrow. "Mike, go fetch your sister's skates." When he spoke with authority, he always sounded like a radio announcer, which is exactly what he was. "How would you feel if we'd left your skateboard behind?"

"I wouldn't," Mike mumbled. He hopped out of the car and hustled back to the old house.

They all watched him, each thinking their own thoughts about leaving Moose Jaw behind. Mike jogged back to the car, hopping back in and handing the skates over to Tabitha, who was sitting in the middle seat. They were definitely her skates, but at some point the plain white laces had been replaced with rainbow ones. It was... cool.

"Thanks," Tabitha said, clutching them tightly, surprised by the gesture even though Mike was still smirking. That was Mike—hiding her skates like a jerk, but then also doing something sweet and surprising. He was impossible to figure out, but one thing was certain: being the middle child seemed exhausting.

Mom turned around in her seat and said to Mike, "Michael Murphy, I sure hope this pranksterism stays behind in Saskatchewan."

Meredith, fifteen, didn't look up from the novel she was reading – she'd already finished her summer assignments weeks ago. She took out an earbud. "Cool laces," she nodded approvingly.

Tabitha hugged the skates. She had been ready to move up to the Little Lasers skaters this season. She hoped Summerland had a good figure skating program.

As if reading her thoughts, Meredith gave Tabitha's shoulder a squeeze, "Coach Wanda says the Summerland rink is beautiful, and that Debbie, the club president, is 'awesome'."

Tabitha breathed a sigh of relief. That was one less thing to worry about. It was nerve-wracking leaving behind everything she'd known. But, that's what was happening.

The station wagon was packed with suitcases, backpacks, and other things the family didn't want to trust to the movers—Mom's favorite science books, Dad's ancient radio equipment and some newer podcast gear, and Tabitha and Meredith's skates, Mike's skateboard, and a cooler full of lunch and snacks.

"Let's get on the road, we've got a long drive ahead of—"

"Tim Hortons!" The kids yelled in unison, pointing at the last chance for doughnuts and coffee before getting on the road.

Patrick Murphy caught a small nod from his wife out of the corner of his eye, and put on the turn signal. They were already behind schedule, what difference would 20 more minutes make?

With doughnuts, coffee and cocoas in hand they hit Highway 1 and made their way west. As Mac the Moose disappeared in the rearview mirror, the move really started to feel real. Tabitha watched her hometown shrink and disappear into prairie highway.

As the steady rhythm of the highway lines passed by, and her dad lightly drummed his fingers on the steering wheel along with the radio, Tabitha adjusted her lucky baseball hat, settled into her seat, and let her thoughts drift.

She was sad about leaving her friends and skating club behind, but mostly excited about what lay ahead. Since she'd known for months they were moving, she'd had time to get used to the idea. And also, since it was happening whether she liked it or not, she had decided she was going to like it.

Did You Know? Mac the Moose in Moose Jaw, Saskatchewan, was the world's largest moose statue until Norway built a slightly taller one! In 2019, Moose Jaw made Mac even taller to reclaim the title. Now that's Canadian pride!

Chapter Two

Welcome to Summerland

The Murphys arrived in Summerland as the August sun was setting behind the mountains, painting the sky in shades of pink and orange. The heat of the sunny day still lingered in the air, making the idea of unpacking even more daunting.

"Ladies and gentlemen," Dad announced in his best radio voice, "welcome to the grand tour of Summerland!" He pulled off the highway and guided the station wagon up Rosedale Avenue, narrating their journey as if reading a charming human interest story on air.

"That's Granny's Fruit Stand, featuring the Okanagan Valley's best fruit selection. Over there, The Beanery, purveyors of the Okanagan's finest hot chocolate." They turned up Main Street, past a door with CKSP written in bold letters ("The coolest radio station in the Okanagan Valley!")

and the high school where, "the smartest, most beautiful teacher in the world will soon be teaching science".

Just as Dad's tour was hitting its stride, they turned onto Campbell Crescent, a quiet street lined with maple trees just starting to show hints of autumn red and gold. Their new house stood in the late afternoon light: cream-colored with dark blue trim, surrounded by flowerbeds and fruit trees dotting both front and back lawns. An apple tree stretched its branches toward an upstairs window.

"This is it," Dad said. "Our final stop: Home sweet home."

"Last one has to unpack the kitchen!" Mike shouted, leaping from the car before it had fully stopped.

"Michael!" Mom called after him, but he was already racing toward the front door, leaving his backpack behind for someone else to carry—as usual.

As they began unloading the car, Tabitha noticed a boy about her age sitting on the front steps of the house across the street, intently focused on a sketchbook. He looked up and smiled and waved.

Dad lifted up the doormat. No house key. "Uh oh," he muttered.

Forty-five minutes and one visit from a *very* apologetic realtor later, they were in the house. The door swung open, releasing the smell of fresh paint and possibility. Their footsteps echoed off bare walls as they explored, each empty room waiting to be filled with new energy.

Mike immediately claimed the basement bedroom ("Perfect for my evil laboratory!" he announced, attempting a sinister cackle). Tabitha and Meredith got rooms upstairs, connected by a shared bathroom that would definitely lead to some sister squabbles—but also late-night talks about school, skating, and everything else. Hopefully.

"Mike's not actually evil," Meredith said thoughtfully, arranging her competition medals on her desk. "He's just got a lot of energy."

"He's also not a genius," said Tabitha. "But he *can* be a jerk sometimes."

"Awwwwwwwww," Tabitha turned around and saw Mike at the bottom of the stairs. He'd heard everything.

"A *jerk*??" he called. "Would a jerk do this?" He picked up her baseball cap off the bottom step and left. "Yoink!"

"Hey!" Tabitha shouted and raced down the stairs after him. "That's absolutely a jerk thing to do!"

Mike ran through the kitchen and tossed her hat into the basement. He turned around with a smile on his face. "Looking for your hat, Tab? Maybe try down there," he said, pointing.

"See? I'm helping," he added, as Tabitha went down into the basement to retrieve her hat.

Half of the basement was finished with what looked like a fun place for grown-ups to sit around. A TV had obviously hung on the wall and there was deep carpet everywhere. The movers had put a couple of couches down there and stacked a whole pile of cardboard boxes.

The other half was just a bare cement floor, and against one wall was a hockey net, surrounded by scuff marks that suggested years of practice shots. Must have been left by the old owners, Tabitha thought.

She grabbed her hat off the floor and decided to check on the room Mike had claimed. She put her hand on the doorknob.

"Stay outta my room, nerd!" Mike shouted from somewhere above. How did he know? Did he rig up some kind of warning system? But they'd just arrived! That guy was a real mystery.

As she reached the top of the stairs she saw figures standing by the kitchen door. "Knock knock," the woman said. She was carrying what looked like a welcome basket. Next to her stood the boy with the sketchbook. "I'm Sarah, and this is my son Roger. We live just across the way."

"Perfect timing!" Mom smiled, wiping her forehead. "I'm Kate Murphy, and these are our kids – Meredith, Mike, and Tabitha."

"What are you drawing?" Tabitha asked Roger, pointing at his sketchbook.

"A comic called Kung-fu Ken and the River Blades," Roger replied, showing her a page. "It's about a kung-fu master who's also a hockey goalie."

"Cool!" Tabitha said, impressed by the drawings. "You drew that?"

"Yep," Roger replied with a big smile on his face. Before they knew it, they were seated on the lawn, looking through the sketchbook and then they got to talking about skating. Roger, who was a two-way centre for the Summerland Jets, was showing Tabitha dekes, as she showed him figure skating jumps and pirouettes on the lawn. It seemed like only a few minutes, but as the light started to fade, Roger's mom called him home, and Tabitha went in for dinner.

She couldn't believe it: she'd made a friend. And they'd only just arrived! After dinner, Tabitha went upstairs to her new room. Her room faced west, and through the big window, she could see the evening light dappling the hills. The topmost branches of an apple tree stretched up, dotted with a few bright red apples.

"Your room has the best view of the sunset," Meredith said, mock pouting. "I'm gonna come in to watch it anytime I want!" Tabitha shrugged happily.

That sounded good to her.

Did You Know? The Okanagan Valley, where Summerland is located, produces about 25% of all Canadian fruit! The region is perfect for growing apples, peaches, and cherries because it gets more sunshine than almost anywhere else in the country.

Chapter Three

First Visit to School

The last week of August flew by in a whirlwind of preparation. Mom spent long hours setting up her science classroom, while Meredith seemed content to work on her skating choreography in the driveway in between chapters of her book. Mike disappeared regularly, either with his skateboard under his arm into town, or down into his basement lair.

Every morning that first week, Tabitha would find Meredith already stretching and balancing, practicing on the smooth concrete of their new driveway. "The surface is actually pretty good for spins," Meredith explained, demonstrating a perfect scratch spin.

"Show me?" Tabitha asked.

Soon it became their morning ritual—Meredith calling out corrections while Tabitha worked on her form. "Remember what Coach Wanda always said—shoulders back, core tight."

"Like this?"

"Better! Now try it with your arms in first position..."

It might've looked strange to anyone walking by, but they loved it, spinning and stretching and laughing in the early morning light.

One day as they were finishing their lunch of bean salad and grilled cheese sandwiches, Dad asked, "Who wants to go see the high school, check out Mom's classroom?"

"I'm in!" Mike announced. "I can climb stuff in the gym, and maybe make a volcano explode, and maybe skateboard in the halls, and..."

Dad laughed. "Let's just get to SSS first, and figure out the rest after."

"I need to check out the gym anyway," Meredith said. "Coach Debbie emailed about practice space." She was already in full competition prep mode, even though the season hadn't started.

Mom's classroom was bursting with color and energy. Posters of the human body and a periodic table covered the walls. A model of the solar system hung from the ceiling, the planets swaying gently in the breeze from the open windows.

"Look, Mike," Dad said, pointing to a shelf of science equipment. "Real lab gear. You can do science with it, instead of pranks."

"Hmm," Mike studied the shelf with exaggerated intensity. "*Science*, you call this? It sounds like it might be useful for something, I guess."

Voices in the hallway caught their attention—someone giving what sounded like a tour. "And this is a picture of the Jets after winning their first championship," a man was saying. "That's me in the back row!"

"That's Buck," Mom explained. "Assistant hockey coach and full-time groundskeeper. Former Jet too. You'll hear all about the championship years. I've known him a week and I've heard it at least twice already."

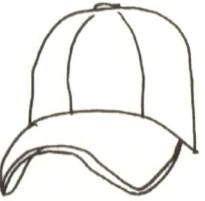

Sure enough, a young athletic-looking man in his mid-twenties appeared in the doorway. He had wavy blond hair tucked up in a Vancouver Canucks stick-in-rink hat, and the easy confidence of someone who lived and breathed hockey. "Mrs. Murphy! Great to see you! Did I ever tell you about my—"

"Championship-winning goal?" Mom laughed. "Yep. But my kids haven't heard it yet."

Buck turned to them with a grin. "Hey kids! Wanna see the school? I can tell you as we go!"

They all nodded enthusiastically. And so off they went, Buck leading the way through hallways filled with early-morning sunlight. He showed them the library, full of unread books, the gym with its gleaming floors, the theater where Mrs. Beaven already had the drama club building sets, and the home ec room that smelled like burnt apple pie.

Along the way, Buck told them all about Summerland—the history, the geography, the best pizza place, the secret swimming spots, and the railway trestle. But his voice got especially excited when he mentioned he'd be assistant coach of the junior Jets this year, alongside Coach Stevens.

"Coach Stevens is a local legend," Buck explained. "Played in the AHL, even had a few games with the Winnipeg Jets." He lowered his voice reverently. "The *real* Jets!"

Just then Coach Stevens himself turned the corner. He had shaggy black-and-gray hair and a big handlebar mustache, with a whistle hanging around his beefy neck. If you looked up 'coach' in the dictionary, you'd probably see his picture.

"New kids? Cool!" Coach Stevens laughed, even though he hadn't said anything particularly funny.

"You bet, coach," Buck smiled proudly. "From Saskatchewan. Two figure skaters and a skateboarder."

"Well, figure skaters have some of the best edge work on ice. Skateboarders... I'm not sure what they do, but a lot of them sure dress funny."

He shrugged and walked away.

"Wow," Buck said. "I've never seen him be that nice to new kids before, you three should be very proud!"

The Murphy kids looked at each other and stifled a giggle. Summerland sure was an interesting town.

As they headed back to Mom's classroom, Tabitha noticed a girl with bright red hair putting up posters for the hockey equipment swap meet. She caught Tabitha's eye and smiled. "Hey! I'm Ami. You must be new—I haven't seen you around."

"Hey, nice to meet you!" Tabitha said. "Want some help?"

And just like that, they fell into easy conversation, putting up posters around the school, then branching out to put up some posters at the post office and on community bulletin boards around town.

"Unngh, second-hand equipment, I would never." Tabitha and Ami turned around to see a tall athletic boy with close-cropped brown hair.

"Hi Derek," Ami sighed. "Not everyone's daddy owns a construction company and buys their baby boy whatever he wants."

He ignored the comment. "Who's this?" he jerked his thumb in Tabitha's direction.

"Hi, I'm Tabitha, I just moved here from Saskatchewan."

"Well, there's hills here now, flatlander. Get used to it." He sneered.

Tabitha surprised herself by replying, "That mountain isn't the only place here that has a giant head."

Ami giggled. Derek rubbed a hand through his buzz cut and then turned around and stomped off.

"He seems charming."

Ami giggled. "Yeah, he's a real piece of work. But he's one of our best wingers. Fancy equipment, but his dad pushes him real hard. Like, *real* hard."

Tabitha nodded.

"I just wish he could chill out a bit. Might help him be less of a jerk."

"Well," Tabitha replied, "Summerland is pretty full of great people so far. One bad apple isn't too big of a deal."

Did You Know? The first organized indoor hockey game was played in Montreal in 1875! Before that, people played on frozen ponds and rivers. The players used carved wooden pucks because rubber pucks were too bouncy on natural ice!

Chapter Four

The Radio Station

As they finished up at the school, Dad checked his watch. "Still got time before dinner—wanna see where I work?"

Meredith and Mom stayed behind as they walked through the park toward Main Street, the late August heat making the shade of the maple trees especially welcome. Inside CKSP, Tabitha's eyes widened. One whole wall was lined with vintage records—sound effects, jazz classics, and rock and roll albums including original Led Zeppelin, the Rolling Stones and Bob Dylan, as well as Canadian classics like Leonard Cohen, Joni Mitchell and The Guess Who. As she explored the vinyl collection, Mike wandered over to the studio and pressed his face against the window.

The control room hummed with equipment, dials and buttons glowing like the controls of a spaceship. At the center, working it all was a tall guy in a brightly patterned shirt with unkempt curly hair and a big goofy smile.

"That's TJ the DJ," Dad said as TJ waved from behind the control board. "The smoothest voice in the South Okanagan."

When the ad reads ended, TJ stepped out with a grin to say hi. "What's up, gang? I'm Teej. I play great tunes, lose pretty regularly at golf, and drive that sweet baby-blue truck out front."

Tabitha giggled. "Hi, I'm Tabitha. I'm a figure skater. You know my dad. And on the end, with his face still pressed to that window, my brother Mike."

"Well y'all, welcome to CKSP. The heartbeat of the town."

"Pretty cool setup, right?" TJ asked, noticing Mike's attention. "C'mon into the studio!"

They crammed into the little broadcast studio and saw all the buttons, the mixing board, the microphone and music.

Mike pressed a red button, "What's up, Summerland?" He laughed.

TJ and Dad looked at each other, then burst out laughing.

"Mike, that went out all across the southern Okanagan Valley!"

Mike's face went beet red. "Uh oh."

"Don't do it again, unless you know what you're doing." Dad was still laughing, but it was clear he was serious.

TJ smiled, "I'll show you how it works sometime, kid. You're a natural." He chuckled.

"Really?" Mike tried to sound casual, but Tabitha could hear the excitement in his voice.

As they headed out the door, TJ called after them: "I'm dropping some Tragically Hip, listen to this classic." He was drumming along to *Blow at High Dough* as they exited the studio, riding an imaginary hi-hat.

"That was pretty amazing," Mike said on the walk home, glancing back at the station. "All those buttons and dials and stuff."

Dad smiled knowingly. "There's a lot more to radio than just pressing buttons, kiddo. But it gets in your blood."

Did You Know? The Tragically Hip, mentioned in the story, played their first show in a high school gymnasium! Many Canadian radio stations have rules—called Can-Con—about playing a certain amount of Canadian music, which helps support Canadian artists.

Chapter Five

First Day Rhythms

All of a sudden—BAM!—it was Monday morning. The first day of school.

Tabitha woke up to the gentle tap of apple branches against her window. The leaves were beginning to turn brown. She raced downstairs into a kitchen humming with the sounds of coffee being made and lunches being packed. Dad jingled his keys and offered them all a ride.

"Thanks Dad, but I think us kids can walk together," Mike said, surprising everyone. "What? Us kids can make our way there." He added, "Don't worry, I'll bring my compass in case we get lost."

At the high school, Meredith dropped off from the group with a quick wave. To Tabitha's surprise, Mike walked her right into MacDonald Elementary and then to her classroom. Mike strode straight up to Ms. Coster, introducing himself with the same confidence he'd shown at the radio station.

"What did you say to her?" Tabitha asked afterward, half-worried he was setting up some big prank.

"I said she shouldn't mess with you unless she's looking for trouble," Mike replied, flexing his muscles.

"Actually," Ms. Coster said, walking up behind Mike with an amused smile, "your brother asked me to look out for you." Mike's face turned red. He gave Tabitha a quick noogie and scooted out the door, nearly late for his own first day of school.

The morning passed in a blur of new faces and names. At lunch, Roger led her to a picnic table under a maple tree where his friends were already gathered. Ami smiled and waved at her.

"I see you've already met our superstar goalie, Ami," he said, pointing to a girl whose lunchbox was covered in cool anime stickers. "That's Benny and Kenny—Benny wears green and Kenny wears shorts in winter, Émile over there is our ace centreman from Gatineau. And that's Shockwa." They all waved and called her over.

"So why do they call you Shockwa?" Tabitha asked the heavyset boy.

"It's short for Shockwave," he explained. "During one of my first practices, I slid into the boards so hard it sent a shockwave through the entire rink. The name stuck." He shrugged, but Tabitha could see he was proud of it.

As lunch went on, Tabitha found herself drawn into their stories about games and practices. The language—dump and chase, high-sticking, toe drag—was like learning a new vocabulary. Even Derek joined them, seeming less of a jerk with everyone else around.

That afternoon, Tabitha headed to the arena with Meredith. They found Ami sitting cross-legged in the penalty box, eyes closed, headphones on, moving her hands like she was conducting an invisible orchestra.

"Oh!" Ami jumped when she noticed them. "Sorry, this probably looks weird."

"A little," Tabitha admitted. "What are you doing?"

"Visualizing success." Ami hesitated, then grinned. "Playing goal is different than the rest of it. I sort of imagine myself as a conductor, and the other players are like the orchestra. Derek's like the violin, and Shockwa, he's got this whole low, steady double bass thing going." She glided as she spoke, demonstrating.

Walking home that evening, Tabitha realized she'd forgotten her water bottle at the rink. "Be right back!" she called to Meredith, jogging back toward the arena.

Through the viewing window, she saw Derek on the ice, a muscular man in a gray 'Benning Construction' sweatshirt was on the ice with him. Derek was firing shots at an empty net. The guy, probably his dad, skated alongside, clipboard tucked under his arm, watching every move with intense focus.

"Again," Mr. Benning's voice carried through the glass. "Harder this time."

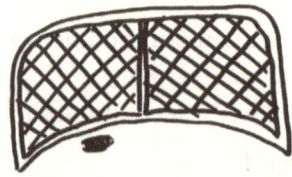

Derek's next shot went wide. He retrieved the puck, skating with short, choppy strides.

"What did I tell you about following through?" Mr. Benning demonstrated the proper form, his clipboard never leaving his grip. "Twenty more minutes, then homework."

Tabitha watched Derek line up another shot, his shoulders tensed up. His tough-guy demeanour was nowhere in sight. He just looked like an unhappy kid.

Did You Know? Figure skates and hockey skates are quite different! Figure skates have longer blades with toe picks for jumps, while hockey skates have shorter, curved blades for quick turns and stops.

Chapter Six

Saturday at the Rink

"Pancakes are ready!" Mom called out as she set down a plate with towering stacks of pancakes in the center of the table.

Tabitha had just finished setting the table when Mike appeared, snatching a pancake off her plate as he walked by. "Delicious! Thanks Tabitha," he said, though it sounded more like "*Mischchous, brinks abnastha*".

"That wasn't for you," she rolled her eyes, reaching for another one, keeping it well out of Mike's reach.

"Family free skate at the arena this morning," Mom announced. "I thought it would be fun for us all to get out on the ice together."

Dad suddenly became very interested in his coffee cup. "I... uh... have a work thing?"

"Nope," Mom said firmly.

"Well, maybe I can head to the curling rink, chuck a few stones?" He smiled hopefully.

"Of course you can, Patrick." She smiled. "*After* you've skated with the family." Having grown up on skates in Saskatchewan, she never missed a chance to get on the ice—especially with her family. "Everyone's going. Even Mike."

Mike swallowed another impossibly large bite of pancake. "Actually, I was thinking about hitting the skate park, but..." He glanced at Tabitha, then shrugged. "Yeah, okay. I'm in."

The arena was already alive with Saturday morning energy when they arrived. Coach Debbie worked with her skaters at one end while Buck ran hockey drills at the other. Roger alternated between sketching on the bench and practicing sophisticated dekes. Ami was already there too, practicing her splits and glove and blocker saves.

Mike was on the ice before anyone else, moving with the easy confidence of someone who'd spent years skating before skateboarding caught his attention. Coach Debbie paused her instruction briefly, watching his natural stride with quiet interest.

"Come on, honey." Mom glided backward, holding out her hands to Dad. "Steady progress, just keep moving."

Dad wobbled forward, trying to keep a casual smile on his face.

Tabitha clicked open the gate and stepped onto the ice. Immediately she felt at home. There was something about the smell of freshly laid ice that made her happy. As she skated between the blue lines she found herself eyeing up both ends of the rink: the familiar grace of the figure skaters at one end, and the quick, powerful movements of the hockey players at the other, zipping the black disks around and laughing.

Derek was running through some drills, showing off a bit with dramatic stops that sent ice flying. When he caught Tabitha watching, his usual smirk appeared. He began skating backward, picking up speed, coming right toward her! It looked like he was ready to deliver a hip check! As he closed in, she deftly sideslipped with a nifty pirouette and Derek clattered into the boards.

He hopped up, looking surprised. Tabitha kept on skating, the beginnings of a smile tugging at her mouth. That had worked so naturally, she thought to herself.

"Wanna try something?" Ami asked, skating up alongside her. "Hockey stops. They're different from figure skating, but edge work is edge work." She handed her a stick and smiled. Tabitha grabbed it and placed the blade on the ice.

"Alright, look at that!" Ami laughed. "You're a natural."

The soft classical music playing over the speakers faded out, replaced by the opening riffs of a Tragically Hip song Tabitha recognized from the radio station. She noticed how the whole rink seemed to find new energy in the change of rhythm.

Tabitha and Ami, along with Roger worked on some basic hockey skills. It was hard, but there was something about the stick, the puck, the skating that felt right. After half an hour of hockey, the buzzer sounded, signaling that open skating was finished and the Zamboni was going to come out to clean the ice.

Just then, a crash made everyone turn. Dad had somehow ended up in the hockey net and toppled it over. "Ha! Just like I planned," he called loudly. "*This* is how they do it in the big leagues!"

"You should come to practice sometime," Buck suggested casually as Tabitha handed back the stick she'd been using. "Tuesdays and Thursdays."

"Thanks," Tabitha said. "Maybe I will." The idea sent a little thrill through her.

As everyone unlaced their skates, Dad's gaze kept drifting to the curling club door next to the arena's main entrance.

"Go on," Mom smiled. "Get in a couple of ends, we'll see you at home."

"Let's watch!" Mike suggested. The kids had never seen their dad curl before.

Through the viewing window, they watched as Dad stepped onto the curling sheet with perfect balance, transforming before their eyes. He settled into the hack, pushed off with practiced grace, and released a stone that curled perfectly around a guard to tap out the opponent's rock.

"Holy smokes!" Mike pressed his face against the glass. "Dad's actually good at something on ice!"

"Twenty years ago, he was Saskatchewan's junior curling champion," Mom said proudly. "How did you think we met?"

"Really?" Tabitha's eyes widened. "How come you never told us?"

"Some dreams you put on pause when you start a family and move around for work," Mom said, watching Dad line up another shot. "But pause doesn't mean forever."

Did You Know? The first goalie mask wasn't used in the NHL until 1959. Jacques Plante of the Montreal Canadiens started wearing one after getting hit in the face with a puck. Now, no goalie would ever play without one!

Chapter Seven

The View from Above

The morning after the family skate, Tabitha lay in bed watching apple branches tap against her window. She heard her dad and Mike leave for the radio station—Dad was showing Mike some broadcasting basics. Meredith had left early for figure skating practice.

"Want to go for a walk?" Mom asked, poking her head into Tabitha's room. She was already wearing her hiking shorts and a bandana. "Perfect morning for Giant's Head."

The trail up Giant's Head Mountain started just a few blocks from their house. As they began climbing, Mom pointed out the different fruit trees in the orchards below—the peaches, plums and apples waiting to be picked. The morning air was crisp and clean, carrying the scent of late summer and the sounds of an active town going about its business.

"I used to go hiking with your grandma most Saturdays when I was your age," Mom said, smiling at the memory. "Course, there's no mountains out in Saskatchewan."

"No, but there's lots of um, *flat* beauty there," Tabitha giggled.

Her mom slapped her playfully on the arm. They walked in happy silence for a few minutes.

"What I love most about hiking is that it's the best way to clear your head when you've got big things to think about," Mom said.

"Who says I'm thinking about big things?" Tabitha asked, but she was thinking... is it that obvious?

"Just a hunch," Mom said with a knowing smile. "I've been watching you at the arena this week. The way you watch both ends of the rink, like you're not sure which direction to go."

Tabitha was quiet.

"When I was at university, I had a chance to go on tour with The Raclettes. Singing and playing guitar, touring the country's bars, basements and curling clubs."

"Did you do it?" Tabitha asked. She loved hearing her mom talk about her days as an independent musician.

"Oh, you bet. I had to try it. But in the end it wasn't right for me, so I ended up getting my science degree and doing more teaching, and now that's what I do... It was a great summer though." She smiled. "It's always worth trying the things we're excited about. It may lead somewhere, or it may not. But the journey is what makes it worthwhile."

They stopped at a viewpoint to catch their breath. Below them, Summerland spread out like a map. The arena's white roof gleamed in the morning sun, and Tabitha thought about yesterday—how natural it had felt to try those hockey stops.

Mom pulled a water bottle from her backpack, along with a small paperback book that fell onto the rocky outcrop. Tabitha picked it up. "Motion Science: Movement in the Real World" she read aloud, noticing the author's name. "By Dr. Linda Chen."

"One of my favorite science writers," Mom said, taking the book back with a smile. "She explains complicated physics in ways anyone can understand. Her chapter on ice and friction is fascinating—talks about everything from skating to curling."

Tabitha gazed out at the view again. "I still can't believe how different the land is here compared to Saskatchewan."

"I know. It's stunning."

They both looked down toward the arena. "You looked happy out there yesterday," Mom said. "Trying the hockey stuff. I can see you're really keen to explore it."

"I am, but." Tabitha's voice trailed off. The truth was, she didn't know what to think. Hockey seemed so exciting, but she was a figure skater. Or was she? Maybe her love of figure skating was more about being on the ice. And there were other ways to do that.

Mom sat on a rocky outcrop, patting the space beside her. "You know what I love about teaching science? It's not just one thing. Some days we're mixing chemicals, other days we're studying stars. And some experiments are just paths that get you closer to what you really want to do."

From the summit, she could see all of Summerland—the arena, the radio station where TJ was probably queuing up another Tragically Hip or Arcade Fire song, the park with all of the kids playing on the playground.

"You know," Mom said, "sometimes the best view isn't from picking one side or the other. Sometimes it's from right here, where you can see everything at once."

Did You Know? Summerland's Giant's Head Mountain is actually an extinct volcano! It got its name because it looks like a giant's head when viewed from certain angles.

Chapter Eight

The Big Mistake

Tabitha found Meredith in the backyard, going through her competition routine in the grass. "Your free leg's dropping," Tabitha said automatically.

Meredith stopped and raised an eyebrow "I thought you only cared about hockey now," she said teasingly.

Tabitha shrugged. "It does seem really cool, but I don't know, I'm just confused, I guess."

Meredith smiled. "You'll figure it out. Oh, and thanks for the tip, Squirt."

Meanwhile, Mike had spent three whole days busy in the basement without a single prank. Downstairs he'd been playing old records, but wasn't doing any announcing. He'd just been quiet, and focused. It was very suspicious. He'd even borrowed measuring cups from the kitchen and asked Mom complicated questions about chemical reactions.

"He's up to something," Meredith warned as they headed down to the basement to get their skates. "He's got that look."

The basement steps creaked under their feet. Mike had hung a sign that read "Radio Production Studio (and Evil Laboratory)" on his door, and mysterious bubbling sounds leaked out from behind it.

"Whoo hooo!" Mike's shout made them both jump. His door burst open, and he emerged wearing safety goggles and rubber gloves, holding a bowl of something green and gloopy. "I've done it! The world's first—whoops!"

Mike's foot caught on his headphone cord. The bowl went flying, sending a wave of sticky green slime through the air. They dodged.

SPLAT!

The slime sailed over their heads and landed right on Tabitha's figure skates, hanging on the rack. The white leather was immediately covered in thick, gooey, glittering green slime that seemed to be... expanding?

"NO!" Tabitha rushed to grab them, but Mike held her back.

"Don't touch it! It's still... um... active."

"Active?" Tabitha echoed, watching the slime seep into her skates. After all those early mornings practicing spins with Meredith, after earning them with last season's bronze m edal... "Mike, what's in that stuff?"

"Just normal slime stuff! Glue, borax, food coloring, a little bit of—" He hesitated, his confident grin fading. "Uh oh."

Mom appeared in the doorway, arms crossed. "What happened?"

Mike sighed dramatically. "A tragic miscalculation. The slime... mutated." He shook his head sadly.

Mom walked over and examined the skates. "The leather's completely ruined," she said quietly. "And is this stuff... still growing?"

Tabitha stared at her once-perfect skates, now covered in a slowly expanding mess. Her throat tightened. "Forget it," she muttered, spinning on her heel and heading upstairs before anyone could see her cry.

She sat on the bed and let the sobs come. Through the tears, she watched the apple tree sway in the breeze. A soft knock came at her door. Mike peeked in, looking embarrassed.

"I really messed up," he admitted, sitting on the edge of her bed. "I'm sorry."

Tabitha nodded. He went on, "Tab, maybe this is an opportunity?"

Tabitha shot him a glare. "For what?"

"Well, the sports swap meet is this weekend." He hesitated. "I could get you new skates. I've been saving up money from my part-time radio work. Any kind you want."

"Really?" she asked, starting to feel a bit better.

"Of course. I really owe you." Mike sighed. "Also, Mom said if I don't I'm grounded until college."

Did You Know? Hockey players used to use straight sticks until the 1960s! Then players discovered that curving the blade could help them shoot better. Now there are rules about how much curve is allowed.

Chapter Nine

The Swap Meet

The Summerland Arena parking lot was already buzzing when they arrived early Saturday morning. Families unloaded bags of equipment from their cars while kids darted between tables laden with skates, pads, and sticks. The curling gear was on one side, and there was also lots of figure skate guards and outfits. The smell of freshly brewed coffee mixed with the less-appealing smell of sweaty old shin pads.

Tabitha took a deep breath, taking in the organized chaos around her. She spotted a few familiar faces—Buck, Ami, Roger, Shockwa. She smiled to herself, then looked at her parents, then at her friends down by the equipment displays, then back at her parents.

"I'm gonna play hockey this season," she said quietly.

She said it again, louder this time. "I'm gonna play hockey this season."

This time her parents looked at her. They nodded. "I'm not surprised," Mom said with a smile. "I think it's something you've got to try out."

"I thought one of my kids would want to join curling, but..." Dad shook his head.

"There's still time, sweetie," Mom patted his arm, laughing.

Buck waved them over to his table, where Ami was already sorting through equipment. "Welcome to the swap meet! You getting figure skates?"

Tabitha shook her head. Ami broke into a big grin. "Ha! I knew it! You've got the heart of a hockey player. Awesome!"

"Oooh, the figure skater's eyeing up hockey skates?" Derek appeared from behind a rack of jerseys, smirking as usual. "This oughta be good."

"Actually," Roger said quietly, not looking up from his sketchbook, "some of the best players started in figure skates. Like Wayne Gretzky."

Buck jumped in, "Welcome to the swap meet! Let's get you geared up."

The third pair of skates Tabitha tried felt different—stiffer, heavier, with totally different blades than her figure skates. When she stood up in them, they felt weird, like the opposite of the graceful figure skates she was used to.

"Walk around a bit," Coach Stevens suggested from where he was organizing registration forms. "You need to be sure."

Shockwa, who had been sitting quietly behind the table, smiled when he saw her. "Hey Tabby! This is great news. I'm not much of a skater, so your fancy moves should help raise our team's overall skating ability."

Over the next hour, her gear came together piece by piece, from shinpads to helmet. Parents haggled over prices while kids tried on equipment, the whole scene humming with excitement for the coming season. Even Derek had stopped smirking and was helping a younger kid find the right size stick.

For once, his usual smirk was gone, replaced by genuine enthusiasm. 'That's perfect,' he said, watching the kid practice his stickhandling. 'Just like I showed you.' Tabitha noticed how different he seemed when his father wasn't watching—more patient, maybe even kind. It was a side of Derek she hadn't seen before.

A stick was the last thing Tabitha needed. "Here," Roger said, holding out one that had seen better days but still had life in it. "This one's got good flex for your shot."

"Welcome to the Jets," Coach Stevens said as Mom filled out the forms. "Practices Tuesday and Thursday, games on Saturday. Buck here will show you the basics."

"And don't worry about being new," Buck added, tossing her a practice jersey. "We all started somewhere. Even Coach Stevens was a beginner once."

"That was a long time ago," Coach laughed. "Back when we still had to shovel snow off the backyard rink."

As they were getting ready to leave, they noticed Dad lingering near a table piled high with curling equipment.

"Looking for something?" asked the man behind the table, wearing a Summerland Curling Club jacket.

"Just browsing," Dad said, picking up a broom. "Though I heard the club needs players..."

"Thursday night league just lost their skip," the man said. "I'm Bob, club president. Drop by sometime."

Dad nodded thoughtfully, still holding the broom. He was still nodding thoughtfully when they left the arena.

When they got home, it took her almost 40 minutes to get into all the equipment. Standing in the basement in full gear, she took a few practice steps, getting used to the weight of everything.

"How does it feel?" Meredith asked.

Tabitha adjusted her helmet, grinning beneath the cage. "Different," she said. "But I like it."

Did You Know? Wayne Gretzky, "The Great One," started skating when he was 2 years old! Like Tabitha, he took figure skating lessons to improve his skating skills. Many NHL players have done the same.

Chapter Ten

Practice, Practice, Practice

The next three weeks were a blur of ice, sweat, and slowly improving hand-eye coordination. Every Tuesday and Thursday, Tabitha found herself at the arena, learning the rhythms and vocabulary of hockey. She was already a good skater, thanks to her figure skating training. The stickhandling was another story though.

"Keep your head up!" Buck called, as Tabitha lost control of another puck. "Stop staring at your skates! You don't have toe picks anymore!"

Tabitha looked up. He was right. She was staring at the puck and that wasn't helping. The thicker hockey skates were starting to feel more comfortable, but it was still awkward. And her stickhandling and shot didn't seem to be improving much at all. Nothing was coming together as easily as she'd hoped.

She tried a familiar figure-skating spin now, on the way to pick up her lost puck. It wasn't truly elegant, thanks to the hockey skates it probably wouldn't ever be, but it felt good. She was moving in a familiar way. As she came out of the spin, Derek skated by.

"Heads up, flatlander," he sneered as he whizzed past, chopping the stick out of her hands. It clattered to the ice.

"At least I learned to skate before I learned to be a jerk," Tabitha muttered.

Despite occasional breakthroughs—a clean pass here, a nice stop there—the frustrations mounted. By week three, the excitement she'd felt at the swap meet had faded into doubt. The puck bounced off her stick more often than not, and Derek's smirk grew wider with each mistake.

"I'm never going to get this," she muttered after her fifth missed pass during a drill.

"You will," Ami whispered, adjusting her goalie mask. "Just not today, maybe."

That evening, Tabitha sat alone in the basement, staring at her stick and the practice puck. Maybe she wasn't cut out for hockey after all. Maybe she should have stuck with figure skating, where at least she knew what she was doing.

She picked up the puck, hurled it at the net and missed. It clattered against the basement wall, leaving a small black mark.

"Useless," she whispered, tossing the stick aside.

Did You Know? The first female hockey leagues started in the 1890s! Women played in long skirts and weren't allowed to use curved sticks. Today, women's hockey is one of the fastest-growing sports in the world!

Chapter Eleven

Snarl Power

Tabitha was still sitting in the basement, staring at her discarded stick, when Mike appeared. He picked up the stick, then grabbed a goalie blocker from a box of equipment. The leather was worn at the edges, but it was still functional—just like everything else in the Murphy household.

"Come on, lazy bones," he said, positioning himself in front of the makeshift net that had been in the basement since they moved in. He put on some more equipment and got himself ready. "Show me what you got."

"What's the point?" Tabitha sighed. "I'm terrible."

"You're not terrible," Mike said, tapping the webbing of his glove impatiently with the goalie stick. "You're learning something new. There's a difference."

Tabitha reluctantly picked up the puck, lined up a shot, and missed the net entirely.

"Again," Mike said, his voice uncharacteristically serious.

She tried again. This one was at least on target, but Mike easily deflected it with the blocker, making a satisfying *whap* sound.

"You're shooting like a figure skater," Mike observed. "All grace, no grit."

"That's because I am a figure skater," Tabitha snapped. "Or I was, anyway."

Mike was quiet for a moment. Then he said, "Forget all that. Shoot again, Tab. But this time, stop thinking about all that stuff."

"What should I think about, then?" she asked.

"Nothing. The puck. The gaps..." he shrugged. "Whatever feels right in the moment."

Tabitha lined up another shot, tears were welling in her eyes, blurring the net in front of her.

"I don't even know if I can be a hockey player," she muttered as she took the shot.

Mike caught it easily. "Not bad. Again."

"You already are a hockey player," said a voice from behind her—Meredith. She leaned against the doorframe, still in her dance leggings. "Practice isn't supposed to be easy, Tab. Murphys love a challenge. Now, shoot again."

She did. Again and again. After about twenty minutes of practice and coaching from Mike and Meredith, Mike suddenly leapt up from his goalie stance.

"I've got it!" he exclaimed, eyes wide. "You just need a bit more snarl!"

Tabitha and Meredith looked confused. But Mike was excited now. "You need to let loose, channel those feelings. C'mon, have fun!" He growled—it sounded like a dog imitating a tiger cub—and he screwed his face up into a mask of anger and concentration. It was all so ridiculous Tabitha couldn't help but laugh.

"Now shoot!" She did, and somehow the stick felt a little lighter in her hands; it went right past Mike's glove.

"There it is!" Mike whooped. "Do that on the ice and you'll be scoring hat tricks in no time."

They practiced for another half hour with Meredith cheering them on, and even playing occasional defense. Finally, Mike let her take a break.

Dad was in the kitchen when Tabitha went upstairs. He slid a mug of hot chocolate her way, complete with mini marshmallows floating on top.

"Did you ever want to do something totally new?" she asked him. "Something that scared you a little?"

Dad was quiet for a moment, stirring his coffee. "You know, when I first started in radio, I was terrified. Reading the news, doing interviews—I was awkward and stilted. It was weird because I wanted to be a broadcaster so much." He smiled. "I was scared. But then I realized that being scared means you're doing something you care about. It's a good thing."

He gave her a hug. "Alright, off to bed kiddo."

That night, as Tabitha lay under her covers, she thought again about what Dad had said. Maybe being scared was just part of the process. And a breakthrough was always on the other side of a bunch of frustration.

The next practice had a different energy. Coach Stevens gathered them all at center ice, his clipboard tucked under his arm as usual, but she seemed excited, almost giddy.

"Saturday," he announced, "we play our first game against Penticton." He looked around the circle, his eyes briefly taking in each player, before landing on Tabitha. "Everyone will play."

Tabitha gulped. A real game. She was going to play in a real game!

The puck felt different on her stick now. Not perfect, not yet, but an improvement. Those basement practice sessions were paying off. She found herself making passes she would have fumbled a week ago, stopping more cleanly, seeing the ice differently. She leaned against the boards with Roger and Émile, looking at plays in Roger's sketchbook.

It felt so real!

After practice, as she was untying her skates in the locker room, Meredith poked her head in.

"How'd it go?" she asked.

"Good, I think," Tabitha said, working at a stubborn knot. "Coach says I'll be playing in the game on Saturday."

"Nervous?"

Tabitha thought for a moment. "Yeah," she admitted.

Meredith smiled. "I always get nervous before big competitions. For me, it's part of why I like them so much."

Tabitha couldn't believe what she was hearing. "You like being nervous?"

"Yeah, it means I care." Meredith gave her shoulder a squeeze. "Now hurry up, squirt. Mom made lasagna."

Did You Know? The term "snarl" is actually used in hockey! Coaches often talk about players needing more 'snarl' in their game, which means playing with extra intensity and determination.

Chapter Twelve

Time to Choose

"Bad news," Meredith said, bursting into Tabitha's room early Saturday morning. "The Okanagan regionals got rescheduled. It's the same day as your first hockey game."

Tabitha's stomach sank. She'd been looking forward to watching Meredith compete—she always did her best routines at regionals. And truth be told, she was missing figure skating.

But after weeks of intense hockey practice, this was also her first real game with the Jets, and Coach Stevens was counting on her for the second line.

"You have to go to regionals," Tabitha said quickly. "It's important."

"I can skip it," Meredith sat on the bed. "But what if Mom and Dad find out?"

"No, I can skip the hockey game," said Tabitha. "There'll be others."

"Great! Thank you, Tabitha!" Meredith looked relieved, then caught something in her sister's expression. "But... this is your first game as a Jet."

Tabitha smiled, but she was feeling awful. This was her chance to hit the rink as a Jet. She didn't want to miss either event.

"Aaaaaaaaahhhhh!" Tabitha screamed. Meredith jumped.

"Sorry, I just needed to let off some steam," Tabitha smiled.

"What's all the yelling about?" Mike appeared in the doorway, headphones around his neck. "Some of us are trying to sleep in here."

"It's nine-thirty," Meredith pointed out.

"Exactly. A true evil genius doesn't really get going until noon."

But once they explained the situation, Mike got a gleam in his eye—it usually meant trouble, but occasionally he had a good idea. "So do both," he suggested, like it was the most obvious thing in the world. "Plus, I've been working on some stuff at the station... maybe we could do something cool with it?"

Meredith's tournament started at 11 am. Tabitha's game started at 2 pm. It was going to be tight.

Meredith's first program was great, though she looked a little rusty. Tabitha could still tell what the best figure skating looked like. And she knew Meredith had better. Luckily she came out much better in the second round, and her moves started to take on the old Meredith gracefulness. "Right on," Tabitha thought.

"And that, folks, was Meredith Murphy with a stunning performance," Dad announced into his phone, while Mike captured it all. "Let's see what the judges say... Yes! Personal best score!"

"Dad, what time is it?" Tabitha asked.

"One o'clock," he replied. "Oh gosh! It's one o'clock!"

They barely had time for congratulations before racing back to Summerland. Meredith and Mom stayed behind to finish up. They'd have to catch a ride back with Coach Debbie.

Tabitha kept watching the clock on the car, seeing it change to 1:40 pm as they pulled into the arena parking lot.

"Watch the stick!" Mike yelped as it nearly caught him in the head, as she hopped out of the backseat. As Tabitha rushed to the locker room, she nearly ran into Shockwa, fully dressed in his hockey gear.

"Thought you weren't coming," he said. "But this is your first game, so you should probably play in it."

"Makes sense," Tabitha replied. "But I had to watch my sister compete."

"Figure skating this, figure skating that." Derek's voice had its usual edge, but not its usual heat. "Whatever. Just... good thing you made it back in time." Coming from Derek, it was practically a warm welcome.

Nothing was going to get her down today. She went into the stale changing room, sat down and started unzipping her hockey bag.

Did You Know? The term "hat trick" comes from cricket. In the 1800s, players who scored three times in cricket would get a free hat from their team. Hockey borrowed the term, and now fans throw hats on the ice when a player scores three goals!

Chapter Thirteen

Game Time

"Attention Summerland!" TJ's voice filled the arena. "The Summerland Jets take on the Penticton Pacers. I'm here with Patrick Murphy, and stay tuned through first intermission for something special from young Michael Murphy!" The game was being broadcast live on CKSP, reaching all across town and beyond.

In the locker room, Tabitha tried to calm her pre-game jitters by taking some deep breaths. Coach Stevens gathered the team for their final huddle. "Alright Jets, this is what we've been practicing for. Play hard, play fair, and most importantly—have fun out there." He turned to their captain. "Derek?"

Derek stood, looking focused. "Remember: we're a team. On the ice, we're all Jets. So let's play like Jets!"

"Full speed ahead! Pew pew pew!" Roger's laser sounds made everyone laugh, breaking the tension as they headed out to take the ice.

The game started fast. Penticton was good—really good. Their passes connected perfectly, and when the Jets got the puck, the Pacers gave them no room to move. The first goal came early when Shockwa lost the puck in their own end, and Penticton scored before anyone could react. 1-0 visitors.

"We'll get it back!" Kenny shouted from the bench, and they did—Roger slipping through the defense for one of his slick breakaway goals. But Penticton kept coming, trapping the Jets in their zone and scoring again. By first intermission, it was 2-1 Pacers.

Mike worked the crowd during the break, interviewing parents, coaches, and even Ralphie the skate sharpener.

He had everyone smiling and laughing, making it sound like he'd been doing radio his whole life. When the buzzer called players back to the ice, you could tell people wanted to hear more.

Back on the ice, something clicked for Tabitha. The game suddenly made sense—not just the plays and passes, but how everything worked together. Halfway through the period, she found herself in perfect position as Derek's aggressive forecheck knocked the puck loose.

She heard Buck's voice in her head: one-two, pass-shoot. The defender came at her hard, but she spun away—the same move from practice, but this time with the puck. It stayed on her stick! She wasn't thinking now. She growled. Then, she shot. The goalie never saw it coming.

The crowd erupted as her dad's voice boomed over the speakers: "GOOOAAAL scored by number 13, Ta-bitha Mur-phy! " Through the glass, she saw Meredith jumping up and down, Mom wiping at her eyes.

Her first real goal! In her first real game.

The third period was back and forth. The Jets scored twice more—Shockwa's big slapshot and Roger finishing a nice pass from Derek. But Penticton matched them goal for goal. With a minute left, they were down 5-4.

Coach Stevens pulled Ami for an extra attacker and pointed at Tabitha. "Get out there, kid." His mustache twitched with what might have been a smile. Derek dug the puck free along the boards and did something unexpected—he passed back to Tabitha instead of shooting. "Smart hockey!" Coach called from the bench.

With thirty seconds left, Tabitha carried the puck up ice, feeling more confident than ever. A quick give-and-go with Roger made space, but Penticton's biggest defender stood at the blue line. She remembered what happened in practice, and dropped low and spun—just enough to slip past the first defender. The second defender hesitated. She wasn't figure skating, but it wasn't exactly hockey—it was Tabitha being herself.

Kenny was wide open by the net. She slid the puck across, and he deftly directed it behind the goalie. The red light flashed and the horn blared.

The arena went crazy. Mike was jumping up and down in the broadcast booth, Mom was crying happy tears, and

Meredith couldn't stop grinning. Even Derek's dad had put down his clipboard to clap.

After the final buzzer, Dad's voice came clear through the speakers: "And that's the game, folks! 5-5, a thrilling tie. What a showing from both teams. This is Jets hockey!"

TJ's voice joined in: "Your kid was awesome out there." They were both grinning as they wrapped up the broadcast.

In the locker room, Derek caught up to her. "That spin move was pretty cool," he admitted. "Still not sure you're a hockey player for real, but... there are signs."

"Oh, jeez," Tabitha rolled her eyes, but she was smiling.

Derek's face changed as he glanced toward the door. "Uh oh, there's my dad. He hates it when we don't win. I gotta get changed."

But before he could leave, Coach Stevens stepped in, followed by Mr. Benning. He walked over to Derek, who looked nervous.

His dad messed up his hair. "Great game kid. You played with real heart out there." He looked over at Tabitha. "You too, girly."

Derek protested, "But dad, we didn't win."

"Baaah, you can't win them all. Your process was good, that's what matters." He even... smiled?

Derek looked surprised—and happy.

As they loaded up the station wagon, Tabitha felt like she was floating. Her first game, her first goal, and her first assist—and maybe even Derek wasn't being such a jerk. Things were looking up.

"You know what this means," Dad said as they walked to the car.

"What?"

"I'm going to have to learn some new announcing calls. 'Beautiful toe loop' doesn't quite work for hockey."

Tabitha laughed. "Maybe stick to 'GOOOOOAL!'"

"Hey, that I can do." He gave her a side hug. "I'm proud of you, kiddo. Not just for scoring, but for being brave enough to try something new." He turned to the rest of the family. "I think this calls for celebration. Dinner at Zia's Stonehouse?" He gave Mike's headphones an approving tap. "Great work on the broadcast, kiddo."

"Sounds good, Dad," smiled Meredith. "Mom, wanna walk with me?"

"Race you nerds there!" Mike called, taking off running, his recording equipment bouncing in his bag.

"No fair!" Tabitha shouted, chasing after him. "You got a head start!"

"Alright, guess I'll drive the car," Dad shrugged, and looked around the emptying parking lot. There were a lot of faces he recognized now. His eyes stopped at the curling club next to the arena. I'll see you later, he thought.

Did You Know? The Winnipeg Jets, mentioned by Coach Stevens, got their name from a famous World War II aircraft! Lots of hockey teams have interesting stories behind their names.

Epilogue – Finding Her Edge

"And that's your Saturday sports update from CKSP," TJ's voice crackled through Tabitha's radio. At the end, he added casually, "And stay tuned next week for something new with our science-minded morning host!" The apple tree branches swayed in the morning breeze.

Dad was making pancakes downstairs and they smelled delicious. Mom hummed along to the radio while grading papers, Dr. Chen's book peeking out from beneath her stack of assignments.

"Ready?" Meredith appeared in the doorway. "Breakfast then the rink." Sunday morning ice time had become their thing—figure skating precision mixing with hockey power until they were doing the best of both worlds. She'd been playing hockey for a while now, but they still loved to mix the skills and styles.

Roger's latest comic pages were spread across Tabitha's desk, "The Tale of the Triple-Deke Princess." She smiled, remembering how he'd drawn her looking like a superhero.

Through her window, she spotted Derek and his father in their driveway. Mr. Benning demonstrated something with a stick, clipboard tucked under his arm. Derek nodded mechanically, but when his father turned away, his shoulders slumped. Some things took time to change.

"Race you to practice?" Meredith called from downstairs.

"You're on!"

The familiar arena smell wrapped around her as she stepped inside—that perfect mix of fresh ice, leather gear, and possibility. Through the glass, Coach Stevens and Coach Debbie watched the early morning skaters, sharing knowing smiles. Coach Stevens tapped something on a tablet, showing it to Coach Debbie. She nodded approvingly, then skated over to the bench to relay some information to a woman who was standing there making notes.

Tabitha stepped onto the ice, feeling her blades bite into the fresh surface. She might not have everything figured out, but she knew who she was: a Saskatchewan kid who'd found her home in Summerland and a figure skater who'd discovered her snarl power.

As she glided forward, Mike appeared at the boards with a strange contraption in his hands, wires poking out the back. "Hey Tab," he called, "think fast!" He pointed the thing—it looked like a camera, a satellite dish and ... maybe a hair dryer—at her. She heard it beep.

"I'm just testing something... for science!" Then he gave a thumbs up to that woman on the bench.

What was he up to? Tabitha wondered.

THE END... for now

Did You Know? The first hockey pucks weren't black! They've been made in blue, red, and even clear colors. Black became standard because it was easier to see on TV and against the white ice.

Chapter Fourteen

Glossary

On the Ice

Hockey Terms

Assist: When you pass the puck to someone who scores. You get credit for helping make the goal happen.

Breakaway: When a player gets past all the defenders with nothing but open ice between them and the goalie.

Deke: To fake out a defender or goalie by pretending to go one way, then going another.

Edge work: The skill of using your skate blades precisely to control your movements on ice.

Extra attacker: When a team pulls their goalie off the ice to add another player who can score. A risky move when you're behind.

Puck: The hard rubber disc used in hockey instead of a ball.

Slapshot: A powerful shot where you wind up your stick and strike the puck with maximum force.

Figure Skating Terms

Edge: The part of the blade that touches the ice - crucial for clean spins and jumps.

Free leg: The leg you're not standing on during a spin or glide - needs to be positioned perfectly for balance.

Pirouette: A controlled spin on one foot - takes lots of practice to master.

Toe pick: The jagged front part of figure skates that helps with jumps and spins (not found on hockey skates).

The Players

Defender: Player whose main job is to stop the other team from scoring.

Forward: Player who focuses on offense and scoring goals.

Goalie: Player who guards the net and stops shots—like Ami, who sees the game differently than others.

Winger: Forward who plays along the sides of the rink, looking for chances to score or pass.

Gear & Places

Hockey Equipment

Cage: The metal face protector attached to hockey helmets to prevent injury.

Hockey stick: Used to control, pass and shoot the puck - every player has their own preference.

Skate guards: Protective covers for your blades when you're not on the ice.

Bench: Where players rest during the game and coaches give instructions.

Boards: The walls surrounding the ice rink that keep the puck in play.

Rink: The ice surface where hockey and figure skating take place.

Curling Terms

Bonspiel: A curling tournament—what Patrick Murphy was excited to start doing again.

House: The circular target area where points are scored in curling.

Stone: The heavy granite rock that curlers slide down the ice toward the house.

Hack: The foothold curlers push off from when delivering a stone.

Canadian Life

Okanagan Valley: The region where Summerland is located, famous for fruit orchards and beautiful lakes.

Timmies: The nickname for Tim Hortons, Canada's favorite coffee and doughnut shop.

The Hip: Short for The Tragically Hip—a beloved Canadian rock band that TJ plays at the radio station.

Double-double: A coffee with two creams and two sugars—a classic Tim Hortons order (even if it's too sweet!).

A Couple More Things

About the Authors

Julius Dogwood was born in Summerland, BC, before setting sail across the seven seas in a homemade catamaran. When not writing children's stories inspired by his hockey coaching days, he builds small rockets, crafts impossible puzzles, and experiments with exotic vegetarian recipes. A true free spirit, he currently resides "somewhere between the stars and the sea," but his heart remains in the Okanagan Valley.

Ryan Millar is a Canadian-born, Amsterdam-based writer, performer and communications trainer. His books include *The Confident Presenter* (2023), a practical guide to reimagining your relationship with public speaking, and *TAKE IT EASY* (2018), offering essential insights for improvisers that translate to everyday communication.

With an MA in Professional Writing, Ryan designs communication programs for organizations including Google and ING. When not writing or teaching, he enjoys skateboarding and spending time with his family.

About the Publisher

Dashwell Publishing specializes in contemporary middle-grade and young adult fiction as well as high-grade creative non-fiction that celebrates authentic voices and experiences. Founded in 2018 in Halifax, Nova Scotia, Dashwell is committed to publishing stories and practical guides that both entertain and inspire readers of all ages. Their diverse catalog includes:

- *Tabitha & The Jets* by Julius Dogwood (2025)
- *Daft Poems and Twisted Tongues* by Julius Dogwood (2024)
- *The Confident Presenter* by Ryan Millar (2023)
- *TAKE IT EASY* by Ryan Millar (2018)

If you enjoyed "Tabitha and the Jets," please consider leaving a review. Visit ryanmillar.com for more books, info, and to sign up for our newsletter.

Made in United States
Troutdale, OR
04/15/2025